Cacti

NICO VERMEULEN

REBO
PRODUCTIONS

© 1998 Rebo Productions b.v., Lisse, The Netherlands
Published by Rebo Productions Ltd., 1998

text: Nico Vermeulen
photos: Nico Vermeulen and Wim Alsemgeest
cover design: Ton Wienbelt, The Hague, The Netherlands
production and editing: TextCase, Groningen, The Netherlands
typesetting english version: Hof&Land Typografie, Maarssen, The Netherlands

E0097UK
ISBN 1 84053 017 0

Contents

Foreword

If cacti did not exist, the film industry would have invented them, probably for a science fiction production about extra-terrestrial aliens. Perhaps it is the extraordinary appearance of cacti that explains their popularity. You cannot ignore a cactus on a window sill. But for many people, the attraction soon wears off if the cactus does not flower. It is only when these plants are well cared for and bedecked with flowers each year that amazement turns to fascination and the cactus owner becomes a real enthusiast. This book seeks to offer help in this process, with growing tips and descriptions of groups of cacti. We have classified the groups in accordance with the latest insights, since they give an excellent insight into the relationships between species in the wild. The climate and other conditions vary enormously for each area. The successful enthusiast should take this into account, and for this reason we devote a lot of attention to the very diverse climates in the areas where cacti grow in North and South America.

Left: the large, golden-spined balls of Echinocactus grusonii

Below: Epithelantha micromeris *in Mexico, close to rocks in the burning sun*

Introduction

What is a cactus?

No fossilised cactus remains have ever been found, so we can only hazard a guess at their origin. It is assumed they are no more than 20,000 years old and are therefore among the most modern of plants. And they are still evolving. All living beings are constantly adapting.

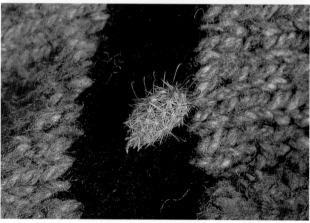

Above: Coryphantha erecta *amongst grasses in Mexico*

Below: the spines of Mammillaria yaquensis *have attached themselves to a pullover, and a loose shoot of the cactus then broken off. In the wild cacti with hooked spines use this method to try and hitch a lift from a passing animal*

Right: in disc cacti such as this Opuntia, *the stem has flattened out and widened to form a disc*

Even the most bizarre-looking cacti once developed from very normal plants with branches and leaves. We know that because there are still living fossils – cacti which have not had to develop so quickly because they grow in areas where further adaptation is unnecessary. *Pereskia* and *Pereskiopsis,* for example, have long stems. Those of *Pereskia lychnidiflora* spread like branches on a tree. This species develops a real tree trunk when it is old. The branches of *Pereskia grandiflora* are only as thick as a pencil, but can reach a height of 24 metres. They carry leaves 10 to 20 centimetres long with a little tuft of spines on top.

Spines make cacti unique

Roses do not have spines – they have thorns. These are pointed outgrowths on the bark. Gorse bushes have thorns on their branches, which are adapted branch ends. Only on cacti do we find real spines. The leaves have been transformed into spines. Just like leaves, they are pushed outwards from a vegetative point. The speed at which this takes place depends on the vegetative conditions. On favourable days, a longer length of spine will grow than on unfavourable days. During the night, growth practically comes to a standstill. In some cacti, a little ridge is then formed, so that the day's growth can be measured from the parts in between. This ridge forms, as it were, a "day ring", similar to the annual rings in trees. The "day rings" mainly occur in *Stenocactus* (formerly *Echinofossulocactus)* and *Ferocactus.* If you cut a spine from each of two plants which have formed during approximately the same period, you can compare them and see a striking similarity in the ribbed pattern. Each pattern forms a sort of barcode. Good days are represented by broad bands, and bad ones by narrow bands.

Adaptation to drought

Pereskia grandiflora is naturally found in areas of Brazil that are not too dry. It is not difficult to imagine what must have happened to these ancient cacti in dryer areas – as the climate got dryer, the plant needed to decrease its leaf surface in order to combat evaporation. The leaves are thicker and smaller in *Pereskiopsis* than in *Pereskia.* If it becomes even dryer, the plant is better off with no leaves at all. They were therefore shed or transformed into other useful organs – spines.

The branches took over the task of converting sunlight into energy. The bark is green. In even dryer areas, even long, leafless branches may dry out. The plant benefits from swollen, thick twigs, that can hold a lot of moisture. Plants containing

Two spines of Stenocactus crispatus (Echinofossulocactus lancifer). *They come from two different plants, but you can clearly see that they were formed in the same period. The bar code is exactly the same.*

The spines of Pelecyphora aselliformis *can absorb droplets of water*

sap are called succulents. Disc-shaped and columnar cacti have succulent, swollen branches. But
in the very driest areas of all, even that is not
enough. The cacti have evolved and developed
further to become champions of the desert.

The content/surface ratio can be decreased even
further by allowing the column to contract into a
ball. A sphere has the largest possible content in
relation to surface area, and therefore loses the
least moisture of all possible shapes. This is why
many cacti from the driest areas are practically
spherical.

This did not exhaust the possibilities open to the
cacti. They have shown that they can defend
themselves in other ways against the dry climate.
Plants breathe through stomas in their leaves and
stem. In cacti, the stomas are deep down and
there are not many of them per square centimetre,
so that they lose less moisture during respiration.
Cacti also breathe in reverse. The stoma are only
open at night, when it is less hot and dry.

Stenocereus stellatus by the sea, with branches thickened into columns

Many cacti cover their chlorophyll with a waxy
layer, which further decreases evaporation. Dense
spine distribution also helps, as less moisture is
lost in the shelter of the spines than in the wind.
Spines also create shade. It is not by chance that
the spines frequently completely overlap to form a
screen around the plant, and in many cases they
are white to reflect the sun to maximum effect.

Cacti seize any opportunity to fill the moisture
reserves in their round body. The extended root
system often branches out just under the surface
and ends close to rocks on which dew condenses
during the night, or else they extend downwards
until they find more moist layers of earth. Not
only the roots can absorb moisture, but the spines
can do it as well. Droplets of dew are absorbed
through tiny openings.

When long dry spells really do become too much

A protective waxy layer on Neolloydia conoidea (Neolloydia matehualensis)

The white spines of Mammilaria candida *reflect the sunlight*

Below: most of the Ariocarpus kotschoubeyanus *is underground*

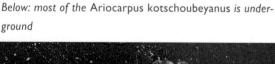

for the plant, some cacti play their last trump card – the disappearing trick. Small cacti with a taproot bury themselves. During the dry period the taproot loses moisture and shrinks, taking the body of the plant into the soil with it.

Protection against being eaten by animals

When an area dries out, less and less plants are able to grow. A juicy plant like the succulent cactus then becomes even more popular with grazing animals.

If they are to survive, the cacti have to protect themselves against being eaten. Most varieties have their spines for this purpose. Sometimes they stab viciously, and in other cases they form a thick trellis surrounding the plant. Then there are the species with hooked spines. Sometimes these help the plant with distribution, when pieces of them drop off easily and are shaken off by the animal somewhere else. In other cases, the hooked spines teach the grazing animals a lesson – as the animal gets stuck and hurts itself trying to struggle free.

Chemical weapons

However, there are also some species of cacti which have few or no spines. They have developed another form of defence – poisons. The body of the plant is poisonous to grazing animals. It does not kill them immediately, but it discourages them from eating too many of the plants. Eating the *Lophophora williamsii* results in loss of appetite and also sends the grazing animal into a trance.

Names of cacti

Nature means movement. All plants and animals are constantly developing, as each species reacts to changing circumstances. The adaptation of one species changes the conditions for other species in the same area, so that they also have to change in order to adapt. Those who seek to classify nature have a difficult job. This is because there are no fixed boundaries. Everything is in flux, moving and merging all the time. Every classification of nature is therefore incomplete, and it is even more difficult with regard to cacti, because they develop so quickly.

Plants adapt to new conditions. If the seeds land in a strange place, normal seedlings will not survive. But some seedlings will often germinate with features rather different from what is "normal". And if that difference now places the plant in per-

Defensive spines on Mammillaria mystax

fect harmony with the different location, then the seedlings have a chance of surviving. Perhaps they are standing in brighter sunlight and have paler spines, which reflect more sunlight. If so, they will not dry out during a long dry spell, while the darker-spined species will. The paler plants cross-fertilise, and paler-spined descendants then germinate.

In recent decades, plant collectors have been sending these deviant plants to Europe, where they were often described as a new species. Unfortunately, people concentrated mainly on the differences between the plants and not on the similarities. Collectors had two good reasons for this – it increases the status of a "cactus hunter" when he discovers new species, and there are a good many cactus enthusiasts who primarily want novelties in their collection, since they are easy to sell.

Botanists who work with cacti today have noticed that many of the taxa which are described are not sufficiently different from one another to merit being called different species. Therefore names are now being scrapped on a huge scale. Now people look at what plants have in common rather than at what separates them. It can then be seen that the taxa which were formerly described as separate species are often the extremes of a single species. The plants may grow in different places and differ from one another, but numerous transitional forms can be found in between.

It is also very important for the serious enthusiast to keep types from different areas apart, so that their different features can develop fully, since these are sometimes very striking and are lost if the varieties from different areas are cross-fertilised with one another. Through these new insights on relationships between cacti it has been possible to distinguish between the varieties and forms. They used to be named in collections as different species, while the enthusiast was not

Left: the spineless Lophora williamsii *uses drugs to defend itself against greedy animals*

always aware that insects were causing cross-fertilisation. We can now prevent cross-fertilisation by keeping related plants which are in flower separate from one another (for example, by putting them in gauze mesh cages).

In this book, the "Cites Cactaceae Checklist" 1992 (complied by David Hunt) is used as the starting point for naming the cacti, in the knowledge that in the course of time many more name changes will take place. To make things easier, common older names are given as well.

The spines of the former Sulcorebutia alba *differ greatly from plants in collections listed under the name* Sulcorebutia frankiana. *But their flower features are identical and they are now all known as* Rebutia canigueralii

Rebutia canigueralii *(the former* Sulcorebutia frankiana).

CHAPTER I

Cacti from South America

Discocactus catingicola

Right: a collection of melocacti

Discocactus

The flowers of *Discocactus* are in a hurry. In the morning a bud appears on the woolly apex (the cephalium). The bud grows during the day (to around 8 cm long), and in the evening it unfolds into a large, white, and often sweet-smelling, flower. At around midnight it is wide open and it then wilts during the following morning. After the seed is ripe, a berry slips out of the cephalium just as quickly, which looks just like the fruit of Mammillarias and Melocacti. But although Discocacti look very similar to Melocacti with their erect cephalium, they are not closely related. Discos grow in southern Brazil and the adjacent areas of Paraguay and eastern Bolivia, usually a few hundred metres above sea level. The area is in the tropics, and is not too high, since the cacti are not used to low temperatures. In our collections they cannot tolerate the cold. Most Discocacti need a minimum winter temperature of 15°C.

Melocactus

Mature Melocacti wear a hat – the cephalium. Numerous small flowers bloom in this every year, hardly emerging from the wool and bristles. The berries are later squeezed out altogether, so that they are more noticeable than the flowers.

For about the first seven years (two to three years in warm areas), the plant grows into a ball or short column (often as large as a football). After that it stops growing and the cephalium starts to form. The body of the plant does not

1 At midday, buds begin to appear in the apex of Discocactus horstii

2 The evening of the same day

Melocactus neryi

grow any more, but the narrower, erect cephalium becomes longer each year. In some species, it eventually stands as a bristly column above the ball.

Melocacti grow in an extensive area of Central America, including the Caribbean Islands and reaching to the northern half of South America (where they are almost exclusively found in low-lying coastal areas). It is always warm there and Melocacti can only survive if they are kept at at least 15°C even in winter. Only some inland species, such as *Melocactus neryi,* can tolerate lower temperatures.

Plants with a cephalium that are brought in from the wild cannot survive this. Melocacti have a very extensive root system, which in flowering

3 Later the same evening

4 At around midnight Discocactus horstii *blooms in all its glory*

plants, finds it practically impossible to recover from damage.

Uebelmannia

With its chocolate brown body and crested spines on the sharp ribs, *Uebelmannia pectinifera* looks like a living fossil. The plant grows in the mountainous regions of southeast Brazil on quartz slopes rich in humus (for it is wet, warm and therefore green there during the rainy season). The plant requires a minimum of 15°C (even in winter), as well as a very acidic soil mixture rich in humus. The three other *Uebelmannia* species require the same treatment.

Parodia

Parodia has become a large genus now that most Notocacti have been included in it. The *Notocactus* itself was formerly divided into *Eriocactus*, *Brasilicactus*, *Wigginsia (= Malacocarpus)* and *Notocactus*. *Wigginsia* (also wrongly known as *Malacocarpus)* forms a group of Notocacti with a very woolly apex. *Eriocactus* and *Brasilicactus* do not have the red pistil and stigma, which, strictly speaking, are typical of *Notocactus*. This is not really a reason to invent a new genus, but it is still useful to separate them as a group, since they present a very clear image – the sharp ribs of plants from the Wigginsia Group with a woolly vegetative point, the flattened balls of the Brasilicactus Group surrounded by innumerable fine spines, and the golden spines and columnar shape of the species from the Eriocactus group with their crooked apex. They are clear images which are useful among cactus enthusiasts.

All these groups, together with the typical Notos (with their red style and stigmas), make up the former genus Notocactus. The species which belong to this genus extend over an enormous area – extending northwards from the cool southern part of Argentina right up to the border with Bolivia and eastwards towards Paraguay and the southern

Uebelmannia pectinifera

Left: Melocactus azureus

Below: Parodia maassii

Parodia magnifica (Notocactus magnificus)

provinces of Brazil. There (and in neighbouring Uruguay) is the probable centre of distribution. Although the areas where they grow are sometimes thousands of kilometres apart, the variation in climate is surprisingly small. In Southern Patagonia it is still cool and it gets warmer as one goes northwards. But there the plants grow on the Pampas, Gran Chaco and Mato Grosso, beautiful names for extensive grassy areas a few hundred metres above sea level. The mountains have been eroded into plateaus in this old country, with river beds in between which transport the precipitation that pours down in the rainy season. In the dry season they dry up. Most Notocacti grow on the slopes of these beds and on top of the flat hill ridges. The lower plains are covered with grass.

Right: Parodia leninghausii (Notocactus leninghausii)

Parodia neohorstii (Wigginsia horstii)

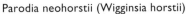

Parodia schwebsiana

Parodia penicillata

Right: Parodia punae

The plants are often partly shaded by shrubs and high grasses. The soil is rich in humus and so does not dry out quickly.

With a pH of 4.5 to 5.5., the soil is clearly acidic.

Parodia haselbergii (Notocactus haselbergii)

These conditions can be imitated even in our climates without too much trouble, making Notocacti among the easiest cacti to cultivate. In the winter they are kept just about frost free, but preferably rather warmer (around 10°C). Then they can be watered from time to time, so that the potting compost is never bone dry. If it dries out completely, some of the roots will die and the plants will be slower to begin growing in the spring. They like to be watered again quite early in the season (March), so that the vegetative point begins to shine with new life. In April-May time, most species are in full bloom. Keep the earth quite moist throughout the summer. In the warmer months they like to be placed outside, without protection against rain – the ideal pick-me-up for plants belonging to window sill growers. They will derive much pleasure from the Notos, because they require significantly less light than many other cacti. The situation is different for Parodias

(except the Notocactus group). Real Parodias are found on high ground where the grassy plains of western Argentina and southern Bolivia border on the Andes. They like a light, airy location that is not too hot. Parodias in the strict sense are among the most beautiful cacti. Their areoles are often very close together, arranged in ribs or spirals. White wool sprouts from the young areoles, from which magnificent spines also emerge. The central spine is sometimes hooked. In the summer, full tufts of large yellow, orange or scarlet flowers flower from the apex. The seeds of a number of species are remarkably small. They are carried to other locations in the wild by water and ants.

Sowing the small-seeded Parodias is a job for people with courage and patience. The seedlings grow so slowly that they cannot be planted out until the second year. A green algal layer sometimes gets there before the enthusiasts. The seedlings will no longer grow in such a layer, so it is all the more exciting if you are successful.

Most parodias are easy to cultivate as a mature

Left: Notocactus rutilans

Right: Parodia comarapana

Below: Parodia ottonis (Notocactus ottonis)

plant, but the large flowered species with thick spines, such as *Parodia microsperma*, often come away from the root. They benefit from a shorter period of hibernation, higher temperatures and rather more moisture during the rest period. If this still does not work, then they can be grafted. For this, use a short, slow growing rootstock, so that the plant remains nice and squat.

Frailea

Fraileas are not often cultivated, and that is a pity, because they are something very special. These plants are between two and four centimetres wide. Since most species sprout, the little heads develop into whole clusters in time. Fraileas may begin to flower as early as a year after sowing. They are the ideal plants for beginners who are sowing for the first time. Make sure the seed is fresh, for it is only fertile for a short period. The large seeds also emerge on plants whose flowers do not open. This symptom is called cleistogamy, where fertile seeds are formed in buds without blooming. If the yellow flowers do open, they are almost as wide as the body of the plant. Fraileas grow in the centre of South America, therefore in the northern range of the Parodias, of which they are distant relatives.

Neoporteria

Neochilenia, Horridocactus, Thelocephala, Chileorebutia, Pyrrhocactus, Islaya, Reicheocactus and *Neoporteria* were all completely different genera not so long ago. Most of these species are now included in the large genus *Neoporteria*, since they are not very different from one another from a botanical point of view. The division into groups gives hobbyists some useful indications, though. The Neoporterias, in the strict sense, can be recognised by their carmine-pink flowers, whose innermost petals do not fold outwards and

therefore keep the flower half closed. The flowers also only appear in the autumn, because, even in our homes, they still follow the flowering rhythm of the southern hemisphere. The buds no longer develop in the cold greenhouse in the autumn. Or

Frailea pumila

Neoporteria jussieui (Neochilenia deherdtiana)

Left: Parodia microsperma

else they dry out, or they survive the winter as pink dots on the apex of the plants and then flower in the early spring when the temperature rises in the greenhouse. These plants require a rest during the summer and want to grow in the winter, even if there is little light – so in fact they are quite difficult to keep.

Left: some former Neochilenias are grouped together under the name Neoporteria taltalensis, *as well as the former* Neochilenia pygmaea

Right: the fruits of Neoporteria islayensis (Islaya paucispina) *are dispersed by the wind*

Below left: Neoporteria clavata

Below: Neoporteria ridus

The Neoporterias which belong to the former genera *Neochilenia* and *Horridocactus*, grow particularly well with average treatment. These plants from the Andes (West Chile) like plenty of light, but they also open their funnel-shaped, pale, flesh coloured or pink flowers in the spring, which jostle with each other at the apex of the plant, if conditions are less favourable. Give them mineral soil mixture and a deep pot for the tap-root.

Echinopsis

The former genera *Acanthocalycium, Chamae-cereus, Echinopsis, Helianthocereus, Lobivia,*

Plant collectors give numbers to their new discoveries, such as Lobivia species LAU459, collected by Lau in Argentina at De Portrero.

Below: the only species that still counts as Acanthocalycium is Acanthocalycium spiniflorum

Setiechinopsis, Soehrensia, Pseudolobivia and *Trichocereus* now all belong to the super-genus *Echinopsis*. This genus includes species which are extremely suitable for newer cactus enthusiasts, since they grow without any problems and have splendid flowers.

All species grow in central and southern South America, against the dry, eastern mountain ridges of the Andes. There they experience regular frosts. Even in collections, the plants can tolerate frost (if they are kept dry). They require a cold hibernation period (below about 7°C) to flower well.

The species from the Trichocereus group are often used as the rootstock in grafting, but also produce splendid flowers if the columns are allowed to keep growing. The caterpillar cactus *Echinopsis chamaecereus* forms limbs the width of a little finger, from which numerous orange-red flowers blossom in the spring, if the plant has been kept very cool during the winter – if need be in an un-heated greenhouse, since this cast-iron plant (although it is sensitive to red spider mite) can tolerate 20 degrees of frost if kept dry.

The Lobivia group is definitely the most popular with enthusiasts. These are cacti that flower by day with brightly coloured flowers in yellow,

Right: Echinopsis chamaecereus (Chamaecereus silvestris)

Below: Echinopsi easily cross-fertilise, giving rise to pretty hybrids; this one is Echinopsis backebergii

Echinopsis haematantha *var.* rebutiodides *has red flowers.*
It is often sold under the false name Lobivia famatimensis

Right: Echinopsis maximiliana (Lobivia westii)

Below: Echinopsis schieliana (Lobivia quiabayensis)

orange and red. In the clearly defined area where they grow in northern Argentina and southern Bolivia, the species gradually merge into one another, so that numerous hybrids exist and it is not easy to tell the species apart. They also cross-fertilise very easily, with the result that all sorts of hybrids can emerge in a collection. Protect plants that you want seeds from using gauze mesh.

The species in the Pseudolobivia Group and Echinopsis Group are pollinated by nocturnal insects and open their flowers towards evening. They are mostly yellow or white, and those belonging to the strict Echinopsis Group usually smell wonderful.

Echinopsis arachnacantha (Lobivia arachnacantha *var.* torrecillasensis)

Below: Echinopsis haematantha *var.* amblayensis (Lobivia amblayensis)

Rebutia

Rebutias grow in the mountains at the widest point of the Andes, in southern Bolivia and northern Argentina. Not so long ago the term Rebutia only applied to a small group of cacti. There were also genera such as *Aylostera, Digitorebutia* and *Mediolobivia,* whose flowers are somewhat different from those of the original Rebutias. These

names evoked a certain image in the minds of enthusiasts. Yet the biological differences are too small to keep them separate. They are now classed together in what I will call here the Rebutia Group.

But there were more changes to come. Botanists noticed that two other genera should actually be considered as Rebutias, too. These are *Sulcorebutia* and *Weingartia,* listed here as the Sulcorebutia Group and the Weingartia Group, because they are quite different from the species in the Rebutia Group. The spines in the Sulcorebutia Group sprout from an elongated areole and frequently point sideways. Those of the Weingartia group are robust and tend to stab. They form an

Rebutia neocumingli *is the new name for both* Weingartia riograndensis *in the foreground and* Weingartia erinacea *var.* catarirensis, *shown behind it.*

Below: Rebutia fiebrigii (Aylostera cajasensis)

Rebutia fidaina (Weingartia fidaiana)

Above right: Rebutia marsoneri (Rebutia krainziana)

Centre right: Rebutia marsoneri *ssp.* Spathulata

Below right: Rebutia pseudodeminuta (Aylostera kupperiana)

ing. Plants that are kept above about 7°C in winter will only flower moderately or not at all. Other than that, cultivating species from the Rebutia Group and the Weingartia Group is effortless. Plants from the Sulcorebutia Group are rather fussier. Many have a taproot, which can easily rot away if there is too much moisture. For this reason, the plants are frequently grafted, which makes them sprout more quickly; whole clusters of plants may form. The bodies become more

impenetrable protection around the already hard body of the plant.

Yet they all grow in the same part of the Andes, at heights averaging 3,000m (with exceptional occurrences at up to 4,000m and down to 1,500m). The fact that southern Bolivia and northern Argentina are in the tropics makes no difference at that height. There are regular frosts, mainly during the dry winter period. We can learn something here for our collections. It is not a disaster if the heater breaks down, at least if the plants are kept completely dry. Low temperatures even appear to be a precondition for rich flower-

Rebutia ritteri (Mediolobivia ritteri)

Left: the former species Sulcorebutia frankiana *and* Sulcorebutia rauschii *are both now called* Rebutia canigueralii

Right: Cleistocactus samaipatanus (Akersia roseiflora) *is very different from the plant which is called* Bolivicereus samaipatanus *in collections*

mornings, since this will reduce the chance of red spider mite infestation. It is mainly the species from the Rebutia Group and the Sulcorebutia Group that are sensitive to red spider mite.

Cleistocactus

Cleistocacti form columns between about 30cm and 3 metres high. They stand upright (such as the *Cleistocactus strausii* with its white bristles), grow horizontally in the wild (*Cleistocactus smaragdiflorus),* or may hang downwards (*Cleistocactus winteri,* better known as *Hildewintera aureispina).* The columns flower richly in old age

elongated and succulent, and there is a greater distance between spine bundles. The plants thereby lose their mountain plant charm. A porous soil mixture should therefore be used for Rebutias with thickened roots. The species with a fine, spreading root system like to be watered generously in the summer. generuIn particular, the species from the Rebutia group, which flower between March and the end of May, can be kept in the summer just like a normal houseplant. Mist the plant from above with water on sunny spring

with tubular flowers, which are pollinated by hummingbirds. Cleistocacti grow in a very extensive area to the east of the Andes, where the spe-

cies from the mountains of Peru and Bolivia (up to about 3,000m high) can tolerate some frost. Towards the east, the mountains level off and the plants are less resistant to the cold. That is especially true of the species from Paraguay and eastern Argentina. It is also better for all species if conditions are not too cold during hibernation (minimum 10ºC), so that the potting compost can remain slightly moist. Plants which pass the winter completely dry find it difficult to get going again in the spring. In Hunt's classification, the former genera *Akersia*, *Hildewintera* and a number of species from *Bolivicereus* are transferred to

Left: Cleistocactus samaipatanus (Bolivicereus samaipatanus)

Below left: Cleistocactus strausii

Right: Cleistocactus winteri (Hildewintera aureispina)

Below: Cleistocactus smaragdiflorus

Cleistocactus, which leads, amongst other things, to the apparently very different former species *Akersia roseiflora* being equated with *Bolivicereus samaipatanus* under the name *Cleistocactus samaipatanus.*

Copiapoa

Copiapoas grow in the coastal deserts of northern Chile. In the summer (our winter), they experience unrelenting heat and withering drought. In the winter, the so-called "garua" takes over – a stubborn cover of mist which hangs above the coastline for months. The plants are totally dependent on that mist for their growth, since it never rains there.

In the summer the sun burns. Some Copiapoas have armoured themselves against this with a chalky-white layer that covers the body of the plant. Plants that we grow from seed here, only become pruinose after many years and only if they

Copiapoa cinerea

Right: Matucana myriacantha

Copiapoa tenuissima

stand in very bright sunlight. They should only be watered when they are actually growing, usually not until halfway through the summer. Some non-frosted Copiapoas are easier to grow and flower at a young age, with characteristic saucer-shaped, yellow flowers. Provide a spacious pot for the thick taproot.

Copiapoas will tolerate temperatures just above freezing, but feel better at a winter temperature of around 10°C.

Matucana

Matucanas grow in Peru on the western slopes of the Andes, but higher up than the Copiapoas. There the climate is completely different. The coastal mist, the garua (see under *Copiapoa*) does not reach the Matucanas. They are dependent on the moist air from the Great Ocean which is

pushed up against the slopes between May and November. Cooling causes the water above to condense into showers of rain. In southern Peru, Matucanas only grow at between 2,000 and 4,000m on the western hills of the Cordillera Occidental, the mountain range which runs parallel to the coast. In the northern part of their distri-

Oroya peruviana

Matucana aureiflora

Right: Oroya peruviana

Oroya *and Matucanas grafted onto* Echinopsis spachiana
(Trichocereus spachianus))

Left: Matucana weberbaueri

bution range, the Matucanas have extended along the valleys to the eastern side of the coastal mountain range. There they grow in the river valleys between the mountain ridges.

The lower down the valleys they grow, the hotter the climate is. Here we find the heat-loving species *Matucana myriacantha* and all the species in the Paucicostata Group which were formerly called *Submatucana* – *Matucana paucicostata*, *Matucana tuberculata*, *Matucana formosa*, *Matucana krahnii* (also called *Matucana calliantha*), *Matucana pujupatii* and *Matucana madisoniorum*. These species require a minimum winter temperature of 5°C to avoid ugly spots. They will be at their best in winter at 10°C. The

Matucana intertexta

Matucana madisoniorum (Submatucana madisoniorum)

temperature should ideally rise to more than 40°C in summer, when they like it really hot.

The other Matucanas from the high-lying, cooler areas will tolerate winter temperatures around freezing point and like cool and fresh air in the summer. Keep the temperature below 30°C. The best place for this group to grow is outdoors. They only need to be covered during long periods of rain. Without cover, they can receive maximum benefit from the ultra-violet radiation and will then develop more attractive spines.

Gymnocalycium

Gymnocalyciums are easily recognisable as a group, although it is difficult to say precisely why. There are, after all, lots of cacti with flattened round bodies full of rounded protuberances and with often substantial, spreading, spines. Is it the transverse groove that many Gymnos have above each areole, or is it the completely bald buds and flowers which reveal at a glance that it is a

Gymnocalycium bruchii

Gymno? They owe their name to those bald buds, in any case – *Gymnocalycium* means the same as "naked bud". Gymnos are typical South American cacti. They occur in a very extensive area, from Patagonia in the cold south of Argentina to the subtropical areas in the south of Brazil and south-eastern Bolivia. In the latter area, they grow in an arid area near so-called salinas, dried up salt lakes. It is there, for example, that we find the chalky pruinose form of *Gymnocalycium anisitsii,* which is better known under the old name *Gymnocalycium griseopallidum.*

The most important area for *Gymnocalyciums* is in northern Argentina and Paraguay. It is also

Left: Gymnocalycium quehlianum

Right: Gymnocalycium quehlianum

Below: Gymnocalycium denudatum

there that one of the best-known species, but at the same time one of the least easy to cultivate, is found – *Gymnocalycium mihanivichii.* The ribs of this species are rather pointed and are usually adorned with eye-catching transverse stripes. Striking elongated flowers blossom from the apex, and these do not fully open, even in broad sunlight. The colour of the flowers varies greatly, from brownish-yellow to pink to white. *Gymnocalycium mihanovichii* like a warmer hibernation period (minimum 10°C), since otherwise the plant can easily die off at the root. Drying out does not suit it either, and it does require some water from time to time during the winter.

Left: Gymnocalycium mihanovichi

Right: Gymnocalycium calochlorum

Below: Gymnocalycium bueneckeri

Most Gymnocalyciums grow at subtropical levels in South America, but quite high up in the mountains. They like fresh air, not extreme heat. They often grow in weathered soil that never completely dries out. The plants should therefore be kept growing rather longer in the autumn, and watering should only gradually be stopped in October. Give them a little water now and again in the winter, allowing them to absorb it from below, and carefully water again when the weather improves in March. Once they have started growing in the summer, they flower and grow best in nutritious soil rich in humus, where they will keep growing if watered regularly. It is then that you can expect them to flower in abundance, with one flower after another blossoming from the apex.

The most sensitive species can be grafted. The others grow well on a single root with overhead treatment. Grafted mutants of *Gymnocalycium mihanovichii* are available for sale. These grow as a little red or orange ball on a rootstock. Since they have no chlorophyll, they cannot keep themselves alive and are therefore entirely dependent on the rootstock.

Previous pages: Gymnocalycium pflanzii

Left: Gymnocalycium baldianum

Right: Gymnocalycium mihanovichii "Japon"

Below: Gymnocalycium saglionis (Brachycalycium tilcarense)

CHAPTER 2

Cacti from Central and North America

Ferocactus latispinus *var.* spiralis (Ferocactus recurvus)

Right: Ferocactus cylindraceus (Ferocactus acanthodes)

Echinocactus

Nearly all globular cacti used to be listed under this genus. Now it is limited to six species which are mainly grown for their large size and spines, since they take a long time (sometimes decades) to flower. *Echinocactus grusonii* is the best-known. This is a cactus which is easy to grow with sharp ribs and golden yellow spines later in life.

Echinocactus horizonthalonius and *Echinocactus texensis (Homalocephala texensis)* are much loved for their rather large flowers, which appear on plants about 10 cm in diameter. But both need a lot of warmth, sun and careful watering in mineral-rich soil in order to keep growing well. All Echinocacti come from the southwestern United States and neighbouring parts of Mexico.

Echinocactus texensis (Homalocephala texensis)

Echinocactus texensis (Homalocephala texensis)

Right: Echinocactus grusonii

Below: Echinicactus *and* Ferocactus

Ferocactus

Ferocacti are not often grown in private collections (unlike their relations, the Echinocacti),because they grow too big for many enthusiasts. Only after many years does the large ball or short, broad column begin to flower. The spines are splendid, and often multi-coloured. This is particularly evident in the spring, when you mist the plants from overhead. The robust shape of the plants is not always a disadvantage. Ferocacti can provide variation in a mixed collection. If this only consists of small plants, the overall effect is rather dull. For this reason, Ferocacti can also often be admired in large, public collections.

Ferocactus histrix

Ferocactus peninsulae

Ferocactus wislizeni   *Right:* Ferocactus pilosus

Above: Ferocactus cylindraceus

Left: Ferocactus macrodiscus

Below left: Ferocactus schwarzii

Below: Ferocactus glaucescens

Ferocactus latispinus flavispinus

Stenocactus crispatus (Echinofossulocactus crispatus)

In the wild they grow in dry, hot parts of Mexico and the southern United States, often in the most scorched spots. So make sure the plants receive a lot of direct sunlight, a mineral-rich soil mixture and a winter temperature of preferably at least 5°C.

Stenocactus

Many people know this ribbed cactus by the name of *Echinofossulocactus*. Most species are noticeable for their many sharp, often wavy, ribs. *Stenocactus multicostatus* has 89 in all, the largest number of any cactus. The many-ribbed varieties have a conspicuously small number of areoles per rib. Indeed, the plants seldom grow to wider than 10 cm, so the ribs are very close together.

Not many spine bundles are therefore required to cover the whole globular body. The spines are relatively long, often flattened, but still viciously prickly.

These species cross-fertilise easily, with the unfortunate result that many nameless hybrids come into being. Stenocacti grow easily, preferably in a warm place in the collection, but should be sheltered from direct sunlight in early spring. After all, in Mexico, they have a rather sheltered existence between grasses and low shrubs. There is also

Stenocactus vaupelianus (Echinofossulocactus vaupelianus)

more humus in the soil there than in other parts of central and northern Mexico.

Astrophytum

Astrophytums are amongst the most popular cacti, mainly because many species are covered with small, white woolly spots. The body of the *Astrophytum myriostigma* plant usually has five broad ribs, so that its overall appearance resembles a bishop's hat. The spineless bishop's hat grows in extensive areas of Mexico. The other species have a more limited range. It is noticeable that the areas where the different species grow do not overlap, except in the state of Coahuila. Some types of *Astrophytum capricorne* grow amongst

Left: Stenocactus crispatus (Echinofossulocactus crispatus)

Right: Astrophytum capricorne

Below: Astrophytum *Japanese multi-hybrid*

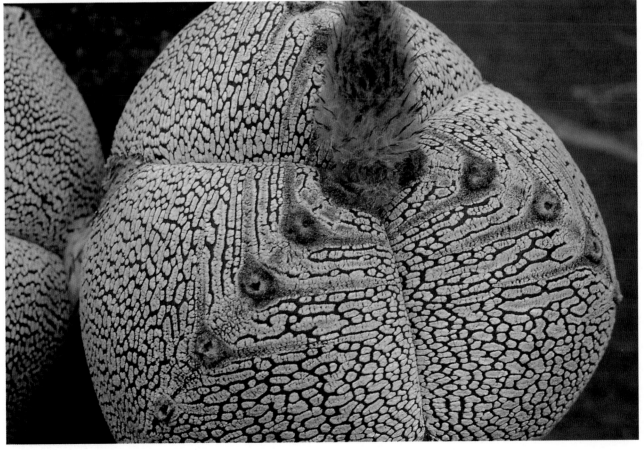

Above: Astrophytum *hybrids*

Left: Astrophytum capricorne *var.* aureum

Right: Astrophytum myriostigma *var.* nudum

Below: Astrophytum myriostigma

the grasses there. In open areas in the same region we find *Astrophytum myriostigma* var. *coahuilense,* which stands baking in the direct sunlight between the limestone rocks. The plant's bark is a striking greyish-white colour due to the innumerable woolly spots.

The other forms of *Astrophytum myriostigma* grow in Central Mexico. There are forms with narrow ribs and with extra-wide *(strongylogonum),* more or just less (four) ribs *(quadricostatum),* densely haired and completely bald *(nudum* and *glabrum),* low plants and columnar ones *(columnare* and *tulense).* And all these forms have been given the names above after their specific characteristic. *Astrophytum ornatum,* with its pretty pointed spines, lives in the states of Querétaro and Hidalgo (not far north of Mexico City). The plants are all columnar, standing up to 1.5 m tall.

All Astrophytums like a mineral soil mixture. Mix a special soil mixture for them, half of which should consist of rough, chalky sand and loose chippings. Water even this loose soil mixture moderately in the summer, and keep the plants completely dry in winter. They do not like the cold. Even in the summer they prefer to stand behind glass, so that they can easily be grown indoors beside a very sunny south-facing window.

Astrophytum myriostigma f. quadricostatum

Astrophytum ornatum

Astrophytum ORMY

Astrophytums can easily be cross-fertilised. If, for example, the pollen of *Astrophytum capricorne* is placed on the stigma of the flat globular *Astrophytum asterias*, then the seedlings which emerge from it are called *Astrophytum* ASCAP (after the first letters of the mother and father plant). The hybrid seedlings have characteristics from both. Some species cannot be cross-fertilised, or this is only rarely successful. Hence the scientist Sadovski was not successful in cross-fertilising *Astrophytum myriostigma* with his variety, *coahuilense*. The latter cross-fertilises particularly easily with *Astrophytum asterias,* which led Sadovski to the conclusion that *coahuilense* is much more closely related to *asterias* than to *myriostigma.* He was therefore convinced that the variety was a totally different species and should therefore be called *Astrophytum coahuilense.*

partly withdrawing into the ground. The species from these desert areas grow slowly and in our climate they are very sensitive to the combination of stale moisture and cold, which can cause the rootstock to rot away quickly. Use a mineral-rich soil mixture by adding at least a third rough sand, gravel or something similar.

Thelocactus bicolor *f.* tricolor

Thelocactus

Most Thelocacti grow on chalky slopes in the Chihuahua desert in central and northern Mexico. It is hot and dry there and the plants are in direct sunlight. They protect themselves from it with very thick spines, or by a waxy layer, or by

Above: Thelocactus setispinus (Hamatocactus setispinus)

Left: Thelocactus schwarzii

The easiest species to grow come from the peripheral areas to the east and south of the desert, where it is slightly less dry. *Thelocactus leucacanthus,* for example, grows in shrubbery as far as Hidalgo, on the southern rim of the distribution range. The species discussed below have one feature in common with *leucacanthus* – they have nectaries above the spine bundles. A sweet

liquid bubbles out, which is drunk by ants in the wild. In this country black rot will grow on the thick nectar. This mould is not harmful, but it spoils the appearance of the plant.

Thelocactus bicolor has the largest distribution range of all Thelos. It grows both in the desert and in moister peripheral areas. It is one of the most rewarding varieties with very colourful flowers which be as large as 8 cm long and wide. *Thelocactus bicolor* f. *wagnerianus* has paler flowers and spines than this species.

If *Thelocactus schwarzii* did not grow in an entirely different area to *Thelocactus bicolor*, it would surely have been counted as belonging to the same species, since the differences are very slight. *Thelocactus setispinus* (formerly *Hamato-*

cactus setispinus) grows in the eastern Mexican province of Tamaulipas, and in neighbouring Texas (USA), along the Caribbean coast and inland. It is undoubtedly the easiest *Thelocactus* to grow, and it is also recommended for beginners. The plant has sharp ribs and flowers at a young age with yellowish-red flowers.

Tough survivors

Mexico (and the neighbouring United States) is thought to have been the birthplace of the first cacti. Nowadays the area is the richest of all in terms of species, and there must have been a much greater diversity in former times. We can deduce this from the large number of relic species, or "left-overs". Once they presumably belonged to genera which contained many species. Although most of them have died out in the last few hundred or a thousand years, there are still some left (in some cases only one).

Thelocactus schwarzii

Some genera consist of only one species. *Aztekium* is an example of a monotypic genus with the only species being *Aztekium ritterii*. It grows in only a few places in Mexico on rocky faces. The tiny seedlings grow extremely slowly and it takes great skill to get them to grow. The same goes for *Strombocactus disciformis* and for *Encephalocarpus strobiliformis*, both from Mexico. The lat-

Thelocactus setispinus (Hamatocactus setispinus)

Thelocactus setispinus (Hamatocactus setispinus)

ter is no longer a monotypic genus, since it is now called *Pelecyphora strobiliformis* and there is a second variety of *Pelecyphora* – *Pelecyphora aselliformis,* also called wood-louse cactus due to the similarity between the adjoining spines and a wood-louse.

Obregonia denegrii is another monotypic genus. This plant grows slowly and is very susceptible to moisture around the rootstock in cold weather. Since the seed germinates very easily, less experienced enthusiasts can also try their hand at this variety. That also applies to *Leuchtenbergia principis* with its extraordinarily long tubercles (up to 15 cm long!). Straw-like spines perch on the end

Left: Ariocarpus trigonus

Right: Aztekium ritteri

Below: Pelecyphora aselliformis

of them and in the summer there will sometimes be large yellow flowers. This monotypic species does not always flower easily.

A few different species of *Epithelantha* are listed, and they are all very similar. Only *Epithelantha micromeris* will remain as a species in its own right. The small flowers are a silky pale pink or white and emerge from the apex of the little plant. It is completely covered with small white adjoining spines.

Lophophora diffusa and *Lophophora williamsii* are very similar, with their spineless bodies with

Left: Ariocarpus fissuratus

Right: Obregonia denegrii

Below: Pelecyphora strobiliformis (Encephalocarpus strobiliformis)

Above: Lophophora williamsii

Left: Collection of cacti with Ariocarpi *in the foreground*

Below: Lophophora williamsii *ssp.* caespitosa

Ariocarpus agavoides (Neogomesia agavoides)

Below: Epithelantha micromeris *with white flowers*

tufts of wool on top. They do not need to defend themselves with spines, since animals that nibble at the plants are quickly sent into a trance by the drugs in the plants (see under "Chemical weapons"). The plants grow slowly but without any problem as long as you only water them during very hot weather (preferably not until May) and stop in time, so that the sensitive taproot cannot rot. The plant partially withdraws into the soil in the winter.

The species from the *Ariocarpus* genus (which includes the former *Roseocactus* and *Neogomesia*) are larger below ground than above it. The rosettes lie with their top just on the surface, at least in the dry Mexican areas where they grow. It is better for us to place them somewhat higher in the pot, to prevent the sensitive rootstock from rotting. These slow-growing plants are grown from seed by advanced enthusiasts. It is a real test of patience, although the plants are much less sensitive than is often thought.

Below: Epithelantha micromeris *with pink flowers*

Confusing relationships

It is mainly with a large group of species from the Mexican area of the US that it has not proved easy to find out the correct name. If it is any consolation, botanists have been trying to do this since the beginning of the 20th century. One expert names one species, another shifts it into a different genus, a third person classifies all the genera differently again, and a fourth joins a number of genera into one. The names of the plants are therefore constantly changing. This leads to considerable confusion among enthusiasts. To help you get to grips with this, we have provided below a list of genera that are clearly closely related to one another, since the species are switched from one genus to the other: *Neolloydia, Cumarinia, Turbinicarpus, Gymnocactus, Pelecypho-*

Left: Pediocactus knowltonii

Below: Pediocactus peeblesianus

ra, Normanbokea, Rapicactus, Pediocactus, Sclerocactus, Ancistrocactus, Echinomastus, Coloradoa, Toumeya, Navajoa, Utahia, Pilocanthus, Thelocactus, Hamatocactus, Glandulicactus, Escobaria, Cochiseia, Neobesseya, Ortegocactus, Coryphantha and Lepidocoryphantha.

Pediocactus

You don't have to heat up your greenhouse for Pediocacti. They will survive the winter. But you will seldom see them, because they are very difficult to cultivate. They naturally grow in the mountains and in the dry high plains of the Rocky Mountains, from New Mexico in the south to the most northerly states of the US. It is sometimes minus 40 there in winter, but the temperature can rise to more than 40 degrees in the summer. There is a real desert climate, where the sparse moisture

Sclerocactus unguispinus (Echinomastus durangensis)

Above: Sclerocactus whipplei

Right: Sclerocactus warnockii (Echinomastus warnockii)

quickly runs down from the hills or disappears into the loose sand. It is also windy nearly all the time, so that the plants are quickly blown dry. By day the sun shines mercilessly on the dry land. It is therefore no surprise that only seasoned enthusiasts can keep their Pediocacti alive, using every trick in the book. It is often too humid in greenhouses in the winter. This is why specialists keep their Pediocacti outside in the fresh air, in a windy spot, but still under a glass cover so that the plants do not get wet.

Sclerocactus

Sclerocacti grow in the same mountains as the Pediocacti, but not so far north. The centre of their range is situated in the southwest of the US. The species that have always been called *Sclerocactus* can tolerate a good deal of frost. The same

is not true of the species that were transferred to *Sclerocactus* from the genera *Echinomastus*, *Ancistrocactus* and *Glandulicactus*. They come from Texas and neighbouring northern Mexico and must be kept out of the frost throughout the winter. These species are relatively easy to grow in a normal greenhouse or cold frame. Grow them in very porous soil and avoid the combination of moisture and cold, which can easily kill the plants.

Turbinicarpus

The new genus *Turbinicarpus* developed with most of the former species of *Gymnocactus* and the genera *Rapicactus* and *Normanbokea*. It is very closely related to *Neollydia*, *Escobaria* and *Coryphantha* and there are clear family ties with the *Thelocactus* and *Sclerocactus* groups.

The Turbinicarpus species grow in the dry areas in the north and north-east of Mexico and neighbouring Texas. They have more or less adapted to a life between dry rocks. *Turbinicarpus subterraneus* forms a vertical radical tuber from which a

Above: Sclerocactus mariposensis (Echinomastus mariposensis)

Below: Sclerocactus papyracanthus (Pediocactus papyracanthus)

Right: Turbinicarpus subterraneus (Gymnocactus subterraneus), *natural growing style*

Below: Sclerocactus uncinatus (Glandulicactus uncinatus)

Turbinicarpus saueri (Gymnocactus saueri)

Turbinicarpus pseudomacrochele
Below: Turbinicarpus subterraneus (Gymnocactus subterraenus), *grafted*

very slender shoot begins to grow towards the light. Once exposed to the sun, the stem thickens again. Most other Turbinicarpi have a taproot which jams itself into crevices. Only a small proportion of the plant is above ground. The spines vary from weak, bent spines in *Turbinicarpus macrochele* to sharp, prickly spines in *Turbinicarpus horripilus*. The latter species, and the others which were formerly listed as *Gymnocactus*, mostly have white, woolly hair in the apex. Buds emerge from here in early spring, and during the spring they develop into splendid carmine pink or white flowers. Pink ones are the most common. The flowers are rather large.

The plants are easier to grow that is often thought. They need a lot of light and are therefore not recommended for indoor growers. They get enough light in the greenhouse or in a pan for buds to form even during the winter. Keep them

Turbinicarpus viereckii (Gymnocactus viereckii)

Turbinicarpus horripilus (Gymnocactus horripilus)

Below: Turbinicarpus viereckii (Gymnocactus viereckii)

dry after the buds form in the spring until the weather turns really warm. Most importantly, do not water them too early, for the combination of moisture and cold will soon cause the taproot to rot away. Species such as *Turbinicarpus lauii, Turbinicarpus pseudomacrochele* and *Turbinicarpus schwarzii* can flower as early as the second year after sowing. Grafting is not neces-

Left: Turbinicarpus valdezianus (Neolloydia valdeziana) *in the foreground with other very similar species:* Mamillaria pectinifera (Turbinicarpus pectinatus) *back right and* Pelecyphora aselliformis *with pink flowers.*

Right: Turbinicarpus pseudopectinatus (Pelecyphora pseudopectinata)

Below: Turbinicarpus lauii

Below right: Turbinicarpus gielsdorfianus (Gymnocctus gielsdorfianus)

Turbinicarpus macrochele

Far right:
Turbinicarpus
knuthianus

Below and right: Turbinicarpus gautii (Gymnocactus
beguinii *var.* senilis)

sary if they are watered carefully. Grafted plants lose their natural densely spined appearance. Grow these plants in mineral-rich soil.

Neolloydia

Neolloydia conoidea (the only species in its genus) is closely related to *Turbinicarpus* and some writers have already classed both genera together under the name *Neolloydia*. However there is a clear difference.

Turbinicarpi have no groove on the tubercles as a mature plant. *Neolloydia conoidea* do have the grooves and the flowers emerge from the axils. In this way, this species is a transition to *Escobaria* and *Coryphantha*. *Neolloydia* grows in Texas and eastern Mexico, where numerous deviant forms occur.

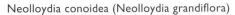

Neolloydia conoidea (Neolloydia grandiflora)

Escobaria asperispina (Neobesseya asperispina)

Escobaria roseana

Escobaria

Escobaria marks the start of the evolution of the most modern cacti (the Mamillarias). The "old-fashioned" cacti carry their flowers on the areole, directly above the spine bundle. Mamillarias flower from the axils. There are two separate vegetative points – one in the areole for the spines, and one in the axil for the flowers and shoots. *Neolloydia, Escobaria* and *Corypantha* are clearly transitional forms, with a groove running from the areole along the upper side of the tubercle. The flowers emerge from the end of this or close to the axil. Escobarias mainly grow in Mexico and the neighbouring southern states of the US. But today these also include the former genus *Neo-*

Left: Escobaria emskoetteriana

Right: Escobaria minima (Coryphantha minima)

Below: Escobaria chaffeyi

bessaya, which means that the distribution range now extends to the most northerly states of the US. By renaming *Coryphantha vivipara, Escobaria vivipara*, the boundary has shifted even further north, for this species even occurs in southern Canada.

The average *Escobaria* is covered in sharp bristles that protect the soft body of the plant. The plants are globular or pointed and usually sprout at a later age, when whole groups may emerge. The flowers are frequently off-white with a green tinge, light pink, rose pink or carmine pink.

The plants in the Neobessaya group tolerate heavy frost (if they are kept completely in the dry). Other species can be treated like the densely spined Coryphanthas.

Coryphantha potosiana

Coryphantha bumamma

Right: Coryphantha poselgeriana *var.* valida

Coryphantha

It is mainly the sparsely spined Coryphanthas that have grooves along the turbercles (see *Escobaria*). Their flowers bloom in summer on the top of the plant. They are rather large, usually yellow but sometimes white, pink or red.

The 40 or so species of *Coryphantha* mainly come from Mexico. The sparsely spined species prefer to grow in the shade of taller plants. The species with a thick coat of spines also appear in the sunniest spots. In our climate, all these species need every ray of sunlight they can get. They like a sun-drenched location in the greenhouse. They are not suitable for the window sill. Give the densely spined species in particular an airy and mineral-rich soil mixture and keep them on the dry side, even for cacti. Sparsely spined species should receive normal treatment for cacti. The honeydew from the nectaries turns black in time through a mould which does not harm the plant, but does spoil its appearance.

Mammilaria lenta

Mammilaria spinosissima

Mammillaria

(Including *Bartschella, Dolichothele, Krainzia, Mamillopsis, Mammilloydia, Phellosperma, Porfiria* and *Solisia*).

Mammilaria schiedeana

Mammillaria muehlenpfordtii

Below: Mammillaria marksiana

The nipple cacti or Mammillarias are not popular with enthusiasts without good reason. They have splendid spines and are therefore pretty all the year round. The flowers are often small and bloom in garlands right around the top of the plant. Other species produce smaller numbers of larger flowers. The best is still to come, particular-ly in the small flowered varieties – the berries. The pointed fruit is often bright pink or red and rather long, and they steal the show by forming garlands in the place where the little flowers bloomed be-fore. Small-flowered Mammillarias are very easy to grow, so that a beginner can cultivate splendid plants in a very short time.

Above: Mammillaria laui *f.* subducta

Above right: Mammillaria candida

Below right: Mammillaria lasiacantha

Below: Mammillaria pottsii

Above: Mammillaria hahniana

Left: Mammillaria pottsii

Below: Mammillaria obconella

Above: Mammillaria glassii

Left: Mammillaria pondii (Cochemiea pondii)

Below: Mammillaria herrerae

Mammillaria pettersonii (Mammillaria heeseana)

Mammillaria microhelia

The 150 to 200 varieties grow mainly in Mexico, but also in some of the southern states of the US, on Caribbean Islands and in northern South America, where the bridge of islands touches the continent. Species from the Caribbean area and from other hot, low-lying areas need more

warmth to develop properly. Species such as *Mammillaria beneckei, Mammillaria guerreronis* and *Mammillaria nivosa* require a minimum winter temperature of 10°C to grow well. Species from mountain areas, such as *Mammilaria senilis (Mamillopsis senilis),* which are

Mammillaria guelzowiana

Mammillaria guelzowiana (Krainzia guelzowiana)

Mammillaria humboldtii

Mammillaria microthele *var.* superfina

Right: Mammillaria nana

sometimes covered with snow 2,500 m high in the mountains), can even tolerate frost for a short time. The majority of Mammillarias can survive the winter at temperatures just above 0°C, with the ideal temperature being between 5°C and 10°C.

Mammillaria matudae

Above: Mammillaria supertexta (Mammillaria lanata)

Left: Mammillaria miegiana

Below left: Mammillaria perbella

Below: Mammillaria longimamma (Dolichothele
longimamma)

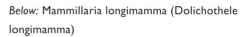

Above: Mammillaria haageana

Above right: Mammillaria rhodantha *var.* crassispina

Right: Mammillaria magallanii

Below: Mammillaria matudae

Nipple cacti will usually grow nicely in the summer, and they should be watered generously. But there are also exceptions to this. Particularly the large-flowered Mammillarias from western Mexico and the southwestern US are very susceptible to a wet rootstock. Use a very airy soil mixture for these species from the *Longiflorae* and *Ancistracanthae* series and those of the subgenus *Cochemiea,* and preferably water them by submersing the pot in water, so that the rootstock stays dry.

Mammillarias are among the "most modern" cacti. This genus is evolving all the time. In most cacti, the vegetative point is on the top of the areole, where the spines also emerge. In Mamillarias, the growing points (vegetative points) have moved to the hollows (axils) between the nipples (tubercles). It is there that the buds develop and the flowers appear.

Mammillaria senilis (Mammillopsis senilis)

Left: Mammillaria boolii

Below: Mammillaria geminispina

Echinocereus

There are about 50 species of *Echinocereus* which are all very different in terms of shape, spines and the colour of their flowers. Some of these species have very thin stems, and they can only support themselves by leaning against branches of desert bushes (the species which were formerly classified as *Wilcoxia),* while others are globular. Some Echinocerei are so densely covered in spines that the plant body is no longer visible, while others are practically bald. The flower colour varies from greenish via yellow to pink and orange-red. With such a diversity of shapes and colours, it is no wonder that some enthusiasts devote themselves entirely to growing this group of plants.

All the species grow in Mexico (the west of the country is thought to be the birthplace of the ge-

Echinocereus dasyacanthus

Echinocereus pentalophus

Echinocereus adustus

Echinocereus reichenbachii *ssp.* baileyi

nus) and the bordering desert areas and high-altitude steppes of the United States. Some practically spineless species are found in the latter growing areas, which largely disappear under-ground during the dry period.

Echinocerei respond well to ordinary treatment, though you must ensure there is fresh air (good ventilation). Keep species with a taproot dry until the first warm days in April, and make sure there is good drainage around the rootstock. The plants grow best in a mineral soil mixture containing plenty of nutrients. In the spring, the sparsely spined species may need protection from strong sunlight. Misting in hot weather reduces the chance of red spider mite infestation.

Right: Echinocereus viereckii *var.* morricalii

Below: Echinocereus poselgeri

CHAPTER 3

Other groups of cacti

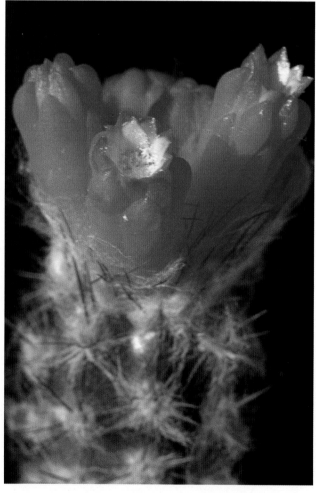

Above: Arrojadoa eriocaulis

Right: Coleocephalocereus aureus (Buiningia brevicylindrica)

Columnar cacti

Most columnar cacti are large and are therefore less commonly grown by enthusiasts. Exceptions are the slender Cleistocacti and the Echinocerei, which do not grow too high. These are widely cultivated. The white-haired trunks are also very popular, such as *Espostoa lanata* from northern Peru, which is completely covered in white woolly hair (but there are sharp thorns concealed in the wool).

The hairs are rather harder on *Cephalocereus senilis.* This so-called old man cactus from Mexico cannot tolerate low temperatures or stale moisture around its rootstock.

The white woolly *Oreocereus celsianus* clearly displays its thorns. The columns up to 2 m high

Above: young Pachycereus marginatus (Marginatocereus marginatus) *plants have white-edged ribs.*

The white woolly ribs can no longer be seen on mature Pachycereus marginatus (Marginatocereus marginatus) *plants.*

Right: Micranthocereus violaciflorus

Below: Arrojadoa

originate from the Andes and can tolerate much colder conditions. They grow quickly without any problems. Put them in direct sunlight.

The columns of *Mila caespitosa* will not grow higher than 15 cm. The name refers to the way in which this plant from the valleys of Peru grows by sprouting. It sprouts in complete walls that flower bright yellow.

Above: Mila caespitosa

Left: Espostoa lanata

Micranthocereus violaciflorus comes from Brazil, but can still survive winter in a greenhouse which is just frostproof. The stems grow to around 1 m high, surrounded by off-white or brown hairs. The small flowers are reddish-violet. The *Arrojadoa* species also come from Brazil. The long columns are just a couple of centimetres thick and sag under their own weight, leaning against bushes or rocks. Towards the end of the growing period, a fluffy cephalium forms on the top from which red or carmine pink flowers will emerge. After flowering, the tip of the column usually continues growing. To grow well, the plants require a minimum winter temperature of around 10°C. *Coleocephalocereus aureus* (syn. *Buiningia brevicylindrica*) needs at least the same temperature with a day-time temperature of at least 15°C. The short, wide column with the cephalium on one side is therefore only seen in greenhouses that are very well-heated.

Harrisia *"Jusbertii"* (Eriocereus jusbertii) *is an excellent grafting stock which itself may flower at a young age*

Pachycereus marginatus (Marginatocereus marginatus and *Stenocereus marginatus)* has no special requirements. It is pretty as a young plant, with the white borders on the ribs, but when it is older, it is much too big. In Mexico it grows to up to 7 m high. At 4 m, *Stenocereus stellatus (Lemaireocereus stellatus)* is also too big for our collections.

Harrisia "Jusbertii" is not known in the wild, but cactus lovers know the slim columns as *Eriocereus jusbertii*, a hard rootstock for grafting, which does not cause the scion to swell unduly. The rootstock itself may already flower at a length of about thirty centimetres, with nocturnal, white flowers, 15 cm long. It requires a minimum temperature of 5°C.

Cacti in trees

Large parts of Central and South America are covered in forests. The trees in the subtropical arid forests shed their leaves in the dry season. Cacti may grow in the ground there against rocks. In the tropical rainforest, they try and climb higher up the trunks to the very top, or take root amongst the fallen leaves in the crown of the giant trees, in a fork between the branches. The cacti from the trees cannot tolerate the cold and must be kept above 10°C in summer and winter. It

takes a lot of energy to keep the greenhouse at this temperature in winter, so the plants are better kept indoors. There they will grow exceptionally well. They need much less light than the globular cacti from the mountains and deserts.

The Brazilian *Schlumbergera truncata* with its flattened limbs is one of the ancestors of the well-known Christmas cactus *(Schlumbergera* x *buckleyi).* This hybrid flowers in the winter with crooked flowers in fluorescent carmine pink or white and any variants in between.

The Easter cactus *(Hatiora gaertneri,* better known as *Rhipsalidopsis gaertneri)* has the same sort of flattened stem features. This plant also comes from Brazil, but it flowers in the spring with orange-red flowers. The secret of its rich blooms lies in the rest period in the months be-

Oreocereus celsianus

Above: Aporocactus flagelliformis

Above: Epiphyllum (Phyllocactus)

Left: Aporocactus x malisonii

Below: Hatiora salicornioides

fore flowering. The plant should then be kept dry and in cool surroundings (but well above 10°C).

The so-called leaf succulents will also flower if treated in the same way. These are hybrids between species from the *Disocactus, Epiphyllum, Heliocereus, Selenicereus* and *Aporocactus* genera. They are sold as *Phyllocactus* or *Epiphyllum.* The sword-shaped shoots, tens of centimetres long, carry very large flowers in early summer, in every colour imaginable. The leafy shoots can become scorched in the fierce midday sun.

The flowers of *Hylocereus,* tens of centimetres wide, open during the night. The triangular stem sectors are often used as the rootstock in grafting. They cannot tolerate winter temperatures below

10°C. *Hylocereus undulatus* are the most common, though these are usually hybrids of other species.

Aporocactus flagelliformis, the snake cactus or whip cactus, grows on rock faces in Mexico. The

Hatiora gaertneri (Rhipsalidopsis gaertneri)

Schlumbergera truncata (Zygocactus truncatus)

Hylocereus

flowers are the same shape as those of the Christmas cactus. They are coloured carmine pink or lilac. This cactus is best grown as a hanging plant. It can tolerate low temperatures and will do best in the greenhouse, where is gets enough light in early spring for buds to form, which flower in the spring. In summer it must hang in a sheltered spot and be misted frequently to prevent red spider mite.

Opuntia

(Including *Austrocylindropuntia, Cylindropuntia, Corynopuntia, Nopalea, Platyopuntia, Tephrocactus*).

There are about as many fig cacti *(Opuntia)* as Mammillarias (between 200 and 300 species).

Opuntia bigelovii

Opuntia articulata *"Papyracantha"* (Tephrocactus payracanthus)

Nevertheless, the fig cacti are not often grown by enthusiasts. There are two good reasons for this – most varieties grow to such large sizes that they are difficult to keep, and they also frequently contain sharp spines and so-called glochids, fine spines with hooks. The glochids remain in your skin if you touch them, where they can cause itching and inflammation. It is extremely easy to grow most fig cacti, since they are incredibly adaptable. No cactus group has a larger distribution range. Opuntias have spread northwards as far as the southern provinces of Canada, and from there southwards throughout the entire continent to the southern tip of Chile.

Opuntia tunicata

Opuntia verschaffeltii (Austrocylindropuntia verschaffeltii)

The tasty fruit and the cochineal beetle ensured that the fig cacti were also brought out of America, to the countries around the Mediterranean Sea, South Africa and Australia. People ate the fruit, fed the shelled discs to cattle and bred beetles on the plants because they contain a precious red dye. But fig cacti are difficult to control. In Australia they ran wild and became a plague in the drier areas.

Fig cacti can be very troublesome for people and animals. The round limbs and fruit of *Opuntia fulgida* detach themselves so easily that it is called the "jumping cholla" in Arizona. It looks as if the plant is jumping on passers-by. At the slightest touch, a person (or animal) will take part of the cactus with them. In this way, it gets a lift to a future growing area. *Opuntia bigelovii* is called the teddy bear cholla, due to its comical appear-

Mammillaria *"Scheidweileriana"* (cristate)

Espostoa lanata (cristate)

Echinocereus (cristate)

ance, but the pale yellow thorns will stab viciously if you touch them. Both varieties belong to the sub-species *Cylindropuntia*, the group with "cylindrical" limbs. They are just over 1 cm wide in *Opuntia salmiana* (formerly *Austrocylindropuntia salmiana*). Fruit grows from the white-yellow flowers. New flowers bloom on the figs, which develop into new little figs, so that whole clusters develop.

The long pointed limbs of *Opuntia verschaffeltii* are often spineless in collections. There are small leaves on the top, which fall off the plant after about a year. Small leaves can be seen on the vegetative point on nearly all fig cacti. They usually fall off quite quickly.

Opuntia ficus-indica is the best-known of the real disc cacti. This variety is often seen in the countries around the Mediterranean Sea. It was brought there for its tasty fruit, while the almost spineless discs are fed to cattle.

Monster cacti forms

These cacti are sick. Normal growth has been disturbed. We call the rock cactus a monstrosity. By nature this *Cereus hildemannianus* ought to be a column (better known as *Cereus peruvianus),* but the vegetative point in the top keeps splitting, so that a convoluted plant emerges. If you sow a lot of seeds, you will come across a deviant little plant now and then. It often dies in the wild, though there are also columnar cacti in the wild where a part of the plant demonstrates monstrous growth. In the case of *Opuntia clavarioides*, it is debatable whether it really is a monstrosity. No "normal" form of this so-called 'black man's hand' is known in the wild. In the border regions of Argentina and Chile, most of the plant is in the ground in the form of a thick root. It has to be grafted for collections.

A crest or cristate shape emerges when the monstrosity grows very evenly by repeatedly splitting in two from the vegetative point. The crest curls while already growing in all sorts of curved shapes. Monster forms almost always have to be grafted to stay alive. Some enthusiasts are prepared to do this. There are even specialists who only collect monstrous cacti.

Opuntia clavarioides

CHAPTER 4

Caring for cacti

Hatiora gaertneri (Rhipsalidopsis gaertneri) *grows and flowers superbly on a window-sill*

Right: artificial morning mist from a plant spray

Growing and flowering

Most cactus species flower every year (and not at intervals of several years, as it is often thought). But they flower differently from other popular plant groups. Fuchsias and geraniums *(Pelargonium)* are in bloom for months on end, while a cactus often flowers for only a few days, or sometimes a few weeks. As a cactus lover, you look forward to the moment when the swollen bud opens one morning and a splendid flower emerges.

How many flowers will open in a given season largely depends on how the plants were cared for the season before. The rest period is obviously important, as is the growth during the previous year. Take the garlands of flowers around a *Mammillaria* – a plant which did not form any new nipples the previous year will not flower. If a row

of new little buds has formed, there will be a single garland of small flowers around the apex. If the cactus grew faster the year before and several rows of new nipples formed, then several garlands of flowers will also open. Cacti must therefore grow well throughout the summer.

Mammillaria elongata ready for sale in a garden centre

A commercial grower's greenhouse

Cactus growing in Tenerife

The limiting factor is the quantity of light. It doesn't take much to get the plants to grow quickly with nutrients, water and warmth, but if there is not enough light, the plant will grow beyond its strength and will end up looking like the cacti that are often sold by commercial bulk growers – the spine bundles are far apart, the spines are thin and the plant is susceptible to diseases, pests and cold. The other extreme is the plant belonging to the enthusiast who grows his plants "hard". The spines are thick and the plant is compact, but it seldom flowers.

The key is therefore to reach a compromise, where the plants grow compactly and healthily and yet still flower attractively. The magic word is light, light, and more light.

A good spot for cacti

In our climate, cacti suffer from the lack of light. Even in direct sunlight, they will get less light here than in the areas where they come from. So always choose the lightest possible spot – right against the window in a room with a southerly aspect, in a cold frame or in a sunny greenhouse.

Window sill growers

Most enthusiasts grow their first cacti on the window sill. This is not the ideal spot, but it is good enough when there is no other option. I have seen splendid collections from many window sill growers. They were all right by the window pane in a room facing south east, south or south west, for only there will globular and columnar types receive enough light to grow and flower properly.

The only cacti that flourish on window sills with less light are those that grow in trees in the wild (therefore partially under the foliage), such as *Epiphyllum*, *Hatiora*, *Rhipsalis* and *Schlumbergera*. They prefer to stand in partial shade during the heat of the day.

Globular and columnar cacti should stop growing in the winter. The quantity of light is less important in the colder months. It is vitally important that the cacti should stop growing – they should not be given any water. If they are kept in warm, dry air, they will dry out. On a window sill with central heating underneath, it is too warm and dry in the winter. Occasional watering is therefore necessary, although you run the risk that the plants will begin to grow in the darker periods. In the winter you should therefore move the cacti into a room where the temperature is so low that watering is unnecessary (preferably between 5°C and 14°C). It is not so important if they end up in a darker spot, because they will not be growing.

In about March or April, bring them back to the brightest window and help them to grow again by gradual watering. Misting the plants from above in the morning using the plant spray will do wonders.

The cold frame

A greenhouse is often said to be the ideal growing place for cacti, but the very best place is actually a cold frame. The plants grow better in this than in a greenhouse. The great advantage of the greenhouse is that you can get in there yourself to keep a close eye on the plants and carry out small tasks.

If your garden is too small for a greenhouse, but you do possess a cool room (as a winter location),

Hundreds of thousands of plants are delivered each year

then a cold frame will be the ideal summer location for your plants. In about April, bring them out of winter storage (see above) to a cold frame. This consists of vertical wooden or glass walls, covered with a sheet of glass or transparent plastic (see "the greenhouse" on making the choice between glass and plastic).

In spring or autumn, the small quantity of air in the cold frame will soon warm up if the glass is in place. It will also keep out the cold overnight and protect the plants from bright light in the spring (extra protection may be necessary if the plants come from a rather dark winter location).

It is in the summer that you derive the most benefit from the cold frame. You can remove the glass completely. All the ultra-violet rays reach the plants. During the night the glass can stay off. The air cools down and in the morning, dew drops will glisten on the spines. In these conditions, the spines turn a very bright colour and the plants grow in beautiful compact shapes.

Some enthusiasts leave the cacti in the cold frame summer and winter. A special winter residence is then unnecessary and the plants gradually get used to the brighter light in the spring. The cold frame must be well heated in winter (for most species). That can be done with electric soil heating cables, combined with a thermostat. Obviously it takes much less energy to heat a cold frame than the much larger contents of a greenhouse. The cold frame is also very easy to insulate. Instead of glass you can insert polycarbonate sheets in the frames, particularly when there is an air trap (a double plate with vertical partitions down the middle). You can insulate the window on the inside with blister padding. A cold frame can also be easily covered at night with rush matting or other insulating material.

The greenhouse

The greenhouse is widely considered to be the ideal residence for cacti. As we mentioned above, this is not actually true, but a greenhouse is very practical. If you still want the benefits of the cold

A collection in a home-made wooden greenhouse

frame, then you can put the cacti outside in the summer. The morning dew does the plants good. You can imitate dew in a greenhouse by misting the plants with a plant spray in the morning. This helps the plants to wake up from their hibernation in the spring.

The greenhouse is mainly for your convenience. You can keep an eye on the plants there in the winter, protected from the weather and the wind, and repot them there in early spring. A collection also looks more attractive in a greenhouse than in a cold frame.

Greenhouses are usually built of aluminium, ready to use, or sold as a self-assembly kit. You can easily make one yourself using steel and wood, though you must take special care to protect wood against rotting, and steel against rust. There are also plastic tunnel greenhouses on the market. These are cheap (although the plastic has to be replaced after a few years), but they are also ugly. The plastic is not completely transparent. The most significant disadvantage of these green-

houses is that they are difficult to ventilate. There are no skylights. Traditionally greenhouses with glass are used.

Check when buying the greenhouse whether short glass or full-length glass is supplied. In short glass small panes are used which overlap. You can cut yourself washing these panes, and they also tear sponges. With full length glass, you do not have the problem of ridges of algae between the overlapping panes.

You can also get thermal panes for greenhouses, but this double glazing is expensive and heavy. The greenhouse must be designed for it. Good insulation is of the utmost importance, though, to reduce the heating costs for growing cacti down from "ridiculously high" to just "high" – and they will always be high.

Polycarbonate sheets with air traps ensure excellent insulation, but this material also has its disadvantages – if attached to the sides, it can make the greenhouse semi-transparent. It is also less stable than glass, so that annoying cracks may

Opuntia tunicata *in direct sunlight*

When buying the greenhouse, make sure it can be ventilated. This is vital for the health of the plants. Make sure there are plenty of skylight windows, from which hot air can escape. These can be fitted with automatic window openers. These cylinders filled with oil open the window when temperatures reach a certain level. You can set the temperature yourself. Check when buying the greenhouse that the windows and door keep out the draught.

A very bright spot is particularly important for cacti from extremely bright areas (such as the southern US and the Andes mountains). Put these plants as close to the glass roof as possible. That can be done using shelves attached to the side walls.

New soil every year

Most enthusiasts repot their cacti every year (except the huge plants in large pots, which can miss a few years). Repotting is sometimes necessary because the pot is too small, but in most cases, repotting is done to give the plant new soil containing enough nutrients and from which the roots can absorb those materials. This is because we alter the chemical properties in the soil by watering. The soil becomes too basic, particularly if we water it with tap-water. That can often be seen from the chalky layer itself that is deposited. The worst sediment is seen if the plants are in earthenware pots, because the moisture evaporates more quickly from earthenware pots and they must therefore be watered more.

For this reason, most enthusiasts now put their plants in plastic pots, which are filled with an extra porous soil mixture. The soil stays wet longer in a plastic pot. Although special cactus soil is for sale in shops, most enthusiasts mix their own soil. This has the advantage that it can be adapted to meet the requirements of the different cacti species. For example, clay is added to soil for plants from the South American pampas, and pumice stone or stone chippings are added for species from the dry parts of Mexico.

appear when it gets colder or hotter in the greenhouse. The advantages of greater transparency, which allows in more ultra-violet light, are offset by the disadvantages of ageing – does not stay as smooth as glass. It scratches more easily and picks up more dirt.

The glass greenhouse can be well insulated with blister padding, which can be fitted in the autumn (to the inside of the glass) and removed in the spring. You will then have an unobstructed view of the plants in the greenhouse from the garden in the summer. Blister padding is similar to the bubble wrap used for posting packages containing fragile items. The air bubbles are much larger on blister padding, which is sold in rolls. Practical materials for attaching blister padding can also be bought. Personally I find the combination of a greenhouse with full length glass with blister padding the best option.

More and more enthusiasts are switching over from soil to so-called substrate culture. In this method the cactus roots stand in a so-called inert material. That might be rock wool, lava pebbles or another material from which the roots receive hardly any, or no, nutrients. The nutrients are dissolved in the water that is poured on them. Substrate culture has some advantages over soil – the roots are less likely to rot, the cacti turn a nicer colour and they do not need to be repotted as often. The disadvantage is that you have to work out your chemicals very precisely and that you have to get your hands on the right materials. Associations of succulent enthusiasts will be able to give you further advice on this.

The pot containing the cactus is removed from the collection using special pliers.

Repotting

The period before growth begins, in February and March, is the best time to repot most cacti. Only plants that already have buds by that time are repotted after flowering.

Shake or knock the cactus from the pot

The soil mixture being prepared

Remove old soil from around the roots

1. Prepare the soil mixture.
2. Pick up the cactus to be repotted. Special tongs prevent you from getting pricked.
3. Shake the cactus from the pot. Wear garden gloves so that you are not pricked.
4. Remove as much old soil as possible from between the roots, whereby the smaller roots may snap off, but the thicker ones are spared.
5. Check the plant for root mealy bugs. If you discover the white creatures or their bluish-white threads, rinse the roots under a running tap until they are completely clean.
6. Partly fill the pot with fresh soil.
7. Lower the plant into the pot and make sure

9. Finally, press the last batch of soil down around the cactus, so that it stands firmly in the pot. Press the soil down lightly.

10. Put the label back on the plant.

Check the roots for root mealy bugs

Gradually fill the pot with the soil mixture

Put the plant in the pot with its roots spread out

Fill the space around the roots with soil

Press the soil down lightly

Label the plant straightaway

that the roots can spread out as much as possible.

8. Fill the pot up some more, ensuring that the mixture goes between the roots. One way of doing this is by knocking the underside of the pot on the work surface between filling.

Sowing cacti

Cactus seeds are not very different from those of "normal" plants. They need moisture and light to germinate. If you scatter the seeds in loose, dry, desert sand, nothing will happen. Only if a seed falls in a favourable spot will it have a chance.

That can be in a rock crevice, into which some dew seeps every morning, or a sheltered spot under a bush. In both cases, the seedling must not be in the burning sunshine at the beginning. If it is it will not survive, since a young plant contains little moisture and has scarcely developed the properties to contain a supply of moisture. Therefore do not treat a cactus seedling as a cactus, but as an ordinary seedling.

Electrically heated propagator with thermostat

Make sure the soil is moist and protect the seedling initially from direct sunlight. These are the two basic rules for sowing. Enthusiasts also use

Aztekium ritterii plants that have just germinated, which are threatened with extinction in the wild

The same seedlings one year later

The young plants after two years

very diverse methods, all of which may produce good results. One sows in little pots of soil, which are encased in airtight plastic bags, another in a window box above the central heating on the window sill, whilst a third uses an electrically heated propagator with a thermostat.

This sowing method is just one of many options –

buy special soil for seedlings or mix a substantial quantity of rough sand with cactus earth (sowing in cocopeat will also do, it is non-germinating). If desired, the soil can be disinfected. This can be done by heating it in the oven, whereby the centre of the earth is exposed to a temperature of least 100°C, or by steaming. Put the earth in a cloth,

Seedlings, mainly Obregonia denegrii

Seedlings which have been planted out for the first time

and put this in a sieve or in the steamer attachment of a rice pan. Bring water to the boil under this. Cover the whole assembly with a lid and let it steam for about half an hour, so that the soil has been disinfected right to the centre. Chemical disinfection is also possible. One relatively harmless agent is Superol, which is for sale at chemists as a gargling tablet for the throat. Dissolve two to four of these tablets into one litre of water and soak the seeding pot in it after sowing.

Actual sowing can be done as follows – fill new plastic pots with the sowing substrate and smooth out the top layer without pressing it down. Scatter the contents of the seed packet evenly on the surface. Depending on the species, you can grow 20 to 50 seeds in a pot with a diameter of 5.5 cm. Label the pot immediately with the name of the species.
Large seeds can be pressed down lightly to bring them into contact with the moist soil. Very fine seeds do not need to be covered. The rougher

seed is covered with a fine layer of the roughest sand or the finest gravel. This prevents the seeds from drying out and makes the sowing pot less susceptible to algal growth.

If you have not already done this, place the pots in a container with some water until the earth is completely soaked. Then take them out the water and place them in the seed tray or the propagator. Cover the tray or propagator with glass or plastic (this creates very moist, close air) and make sure that the condensation that will form on the inside can drain away without dripping on the pots.

Place the whole assembly in a light spot, but away from direct sunlight. The ideal temperature for germination is between 18°C and 23°C for nearly all varieties. Try to keep the temperature between 15°C and 27°C day and night at all times.

After the seedlings germinate, leave the lid slightly open, and as the seedlings grow, slide the lid

Seedlings which have been planted out

across to allow more and more air in. In the case of mould formation, you can moisten the soil with a plant spray containing Superol solution. The plants must never dry out during the first season.

Planting out

Planting out may be necessary if the seedlings crowd one another, or if the soil contains too few nutrients. You should remember that seedlings often grow better close together than in total isolation, so you can grow them "cosily" together, provided that the plants have enough room to grow. Seedlings in a poor sowing substrate must be planted out quite soon. This is particularly important in cocopeat, because it does not contain any nutrients whatsoever.

When planting out for the first time, the seedlings are sometimes still very small and must be handled with care:

1. Set out all the materials (the seedlings, some of them still in a plastic bag, pot and all), a paintbrush or toothpick, a small dish of fresh soil.

2. Squeeze and shake the clump of earth out of the pot containing the seedlings.

3. Break the clump into pieces.

4. Carefully squeeze the pieces to make them smaller until you only have the fragile tap root (with surrounding earth) of one seedling left over. The fine main root nearly always runs straight down and must not be broken.

5. Never pick up the young plants by the rootstock, because they are extremely sensitive to this. Make a small hole in the dish (or pot) containing fresh, nutritious soil with the brush or toothpick and lower the plant vertically into it, whereby the root must fit straight down into the hole.

6. After that, press the soil down lightly around the plant. Keep this dish moderately moist at first and put it in a light spot, but still out of direct sunlight, otherwise the seedlings will be scorched. They are still growing their roots and cannot take in moisture very well.

Set out the materials

Shake the clod of earth from the pot

You can tell they are scorching when the green plants turn reddish.

The plants can still be grown in a partly closed dish for a while. When they are about six months old, you can remove the glass or plastic. They are

now big enough to survive a practically dry winter. If they shrivel up too much, you can give them a tiny bit of water (from below!).

Globular cacti, depending on the species, are large enough to flower after one to seven years.

Break the clod into pieces

Keep doing this until you have a single seedling between your fingers

Work the little root straight downwards into the soil

Press the earth down lightly

Cuttings

Cacti that grow runners can be propagated by taking cuttings. This is easiest with disc cacti, multi-branched columnar cacti and plants that sprout vigorously. Some cacti grow whole clusters of spherical buds which can be twisted off without cutting the plant. The smaller the incision, the easier it is for the cuttings to dry and the better chance they have of taking. Take cuttings mainly during warm and, above all, dry weather. Twist or cut the cutting off at the thinnest point of connection with the parent plant. Use a sharp knife, which has been disinfected beforehand using a cloth containing methylated spirits. If the cut is large, then cut it in a v-shape, slanting from the edge towards the central vascular bundle, since the intention is that the roots will emerge from the central vascular bundle and not from the edge of the plant.

Place the cutting on its side in a warm, dry spot, away from the sun and not close to a heater. After a few days, the cut surface will have formed a callus. The cutting can now be potted. The pot should contain ordinary moderately moist cactus soil, covered with a layer of rough sand or fine gravel. The cutting will "smell" the moist soil below it, and will send its roots there. After a few weeks, you can test whether the cutting has taken by gently tapping it on the side. If it has taken, then you will feel some resistance. The cutting will now grow quickly and can then be treated as a normal plant.

Grafting

In grafting, the top of one cactus is placed on the base of another plant. This is mainly done for species with vulnerable roots. In older books, you will find whole lists of plants which can only survive in collections when grafted. It has recently been discovered that grafting is actually unnecessary if the plants are cared for correctly (in a way that imitates growing conditions in the wild as far as possible). This is why we have given special attention to this area in this book.

In most cases, grafting actually damages the appearance of the plant. Species that are superbly stocky in the wild often acquire a bloated appearance as a result of grafting. Cacti should therefore only be grafted when it is absolutely necessary. By using slow-growing stock such as *Harrisia* "Jusbertii" *(Eriocereus jusbertii)*, the graft will remain in shape better.

Young plants of the globular *Echinopsis* species can be grafted on so low that the stock can be entirely hidden underground after a time.

The columnar *Echinopsis* species, which were formerly listed under the *Trichocereus* genus, have tremendous vitality and cause the scion to swell up.

Grafting technique

The following photos illustrate the grafting of a rare *Lophophora*, which was originally grafted as a seedling onto a *Pereskiopsis*.

1. Choose a short, young stock (which was acquired from a cutting a few some months earlier) and moisten a cloth in methylated spirits or alcohol.

Dampen a cloth with alcohol

2. Clean the blade of the grafting knife with the wet cloth. This disinfects the knife.

3. Cut the top of the stock off level using a razor-sharp grafting knife.

4. Bevel the edges of the lower part slightly (cutting off the top spine bundles).

5. Possibly cut off an extra level strip from the rootstock.

6. Make a level cut to remove the plant to be grafted (the scion).

7. Take the top part of the plant and slide it onto the grafting area on the rootstock. The central vascular bundle can be seen as a ring in the centre of both plants. Make sure that these rings touch one another. The rings are rarely the same size and can therefore usually only touch one another in two places. Slide the scion onto the stock.

Disinfect the knife with alcohol

Below: cut the top off the stock

Below right: bevel the stock

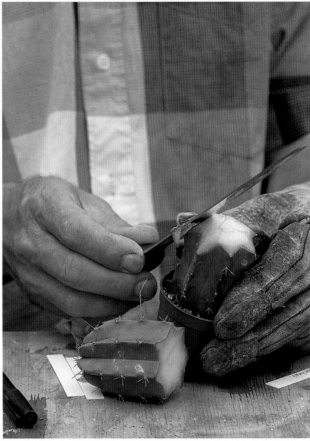

8. Take elastic adhesive tape or strips of stretchy material and use it to attach the scion to the rootstock. Light pressure is enough.

9. To prevent sliding sideways, repeat the process with a transverse elastic band.

10. Place a label with the name of the scion next to the plant and put it in a warm spot, out of direct sunlight.

After a few days, the binding material can be cut off. After a few weeks the scion will begin to grow. If it does not grow or the scion comes away, the attempt has failed. If the rootstock begins to sprout, cut the protuberances off as quickly as possible. Clean the knife with methylated spirits before grafting a new plant.

Left: cut an extra slice from the stock

Below left: cut off the scion

Below: slide the scion onto the stock

Above left: attach the scion with an elastic band

Above: reinforce the scion with a transverse elastic band

Left: place a name tag beside the plant

Grafting seedlings

In the grafting above, a seedling is used that has already been grafted onto the rootstock of a *Pereskiopsis*. This is an excellent way, particularly for slow growing seedlings, of getting them to grow quickly. Despite the fast growth, the deformation caused by "swelling" is not too serious. After a few months, they are re-grafted onto a final rootstock, or cut. In the latter case there is hardly any difference from plants which have grown on their own roots.

Taking cuttings from *Pereskiopsis* is very easy. After a few weeks, you will already have suitable rootstocks. These are between 10 and 20 cm long.

1. In order to graft onto *Pereskiopsis* you need a rootstock, a seedling, a razor blade, a cloth and methylated spirits or alcohol (see photograph on right).

Dampen a cloth with alcohol

Disinfect the scissors with alcohol

Cut the top off the stock

2. Soak the tip of the cloth in the alcohol.

3. Rub the razor blade clean with it, so that it is disinfected.

4. Cut off the top of the *Perskiopsis* and possibly cut another thin slice, if the first cut was not entirely level or smooth.

5. Take a seedling and cut off the top of it. This remains stuck to the razor blade.

6. Slide the scion from the blade onto the rootstock, so that the central vascular bundles make good contact.

7. Take a wooden slat or a glass rod (glass is heavier) and place one end of this on the scion and the other side on a pile of pots that is the same height as the scion.

8. If wood is used, the weight can be increased by placing a second slat on top.

After a few hours, the scion will have grown onto the rootstock and the weight can be removed.

Cut the top off the seedling

Slide the scion from the blade to the rootstock

Below: place a wooden slat on the scion

Right: increase the weight if necessary with a second slat

Cacti which have been seized are cared for in a botanical garden close to an international airport

Keep the growing plant warm, but out of the sun. The top of the *Pereskiopsis* can be potted straight away and will soon start growing again. In the late summer, you can cut the scion, or re-graft it. You can leave it standing on the root-stock, too, but it cannot tolerate temperatures below 10°C.

Pests in the collection

I don't know of any cactus collection without pests. They always turn up somewhere – woolly aphids, root mealy bug and red spider mite. Red spider mite can be avoided by providing adequate ventilation and regularly spraying the plants with water in spring and summer, but you cannot keep the other two pests away for good. There are some enthusiasts who try to do this using poisons. They

endanger the environment and themselves, but while they may win a battle, they never win the war. The use of systemic poisons also puts users' lives at risk. There is a known case of a reputable cactus researcher dying due to the use of systemic poison.

We must therefore learn to live with pests by trying to prevent a real plague from breaking out. When they can, woolly aphids hide in the apex or under the spines of the plants. They prefer to seek out young parts of plants, so that they can suck the juices from them. Outside the growing season, they creep into a safe spot to survive the winter. This is often the rootstock. In the summer, the females are active laying hundreds of eggs, which they lay in a white woolly thread. The small, pink young which hatch out are very active and will quickly colonise other plants, especially in warm and damp weather. Some people think that the young are transferred to other collections by the wind or by insects. It seems more likely to me that the bugs are transferred from one collection to another when plants are bought or sold. The active young are difficult to spot. Woolly aphids do not only live on cacti, either, but on numerous other (sub)tropical ornamental plants. This is where the name of one of the most common woolly aphids in our collections comes from: *Pseudococcus citri* (named after the citrus plant). But fuchsias, bromelias and orchids are other well-known host plants.

Root mealy bugs *(Rhizoecus)* look just like woolly aphids. They have a similar lifestyle, only under ground. There they suck on the roots, which weakens the plant.

You can reduce the likelihood of a real infestation by checking all plants bought and sold thoroughly for pests. It is best to remove them from the pot and to check whether a bluish-white wax is present on the inside of the pot or around the roots (the thread). It may even be possible to see the slender, white root mealy bugs themselves. If this is the case, all the earth around the roots must be removed and taken away. Throw the pot away or (if it is plastic) scrub it completely clean in soapy

Plants grown from seed from the extremely rare Strombocactus disciformis, *a species which is strictly banned from international trade*

water. Also clean the rootstock and roots thoroughly and cut them if earth is left behind on the thinner roots. Pot the plant and keep it away from non-infected plants in the collection.

Woolly aphids can also be found in the rootstock, especially when the plants are resting. The insects hide in the very folds of the plant as it dries out. The most difficult place to combat woolly aphids is in the densely spined apex of a plant.

Once you have found them, they can be dabbed with a brush that has been dipped in a mixture of soap and methylated spirits (dissolved in water).

Protecting cacti in the wild

Some species of cactus occur in such numbers that they are considered to be a pest. Other species only grow in one or a few places. Unfortunately, it is precisely these rare cacti that are very much in vogue. Some collectors only find plants attractive if others do not have them, so it is these rarest of cacti whose survival is threatened. Their natural growing areas are being systematically plundered.

Governments around the world are trying to do something about this by controlling the trade in cacti, and in some cases, banning it. The most threatened species are listed in Appendix I of the CITES treaty. All international trade in these plants is strictly forbidden. All other cacti are listed in Appendix II. They can only be exported with the approval of the country of origin.

Shipments of smuggled cacti are also regularly intercepted. They are seized and housed in other botanical gardens. Fortunately a growing number of enthusiasts will have nothing to do with plants taken from the wild. The real enthusiast will grow the plants himself, from seed.

Index

Glossary

areole	the place from which the spines sprout
tubercle	nipple shaped node with an areole on it
axil	the deepest point between tubercles
cephalium	woolly flowering area in cacti, where the areoles are very close together.
taxa	plural of taxon – the name for a group of plants, irrespective of how and where they are ultimately classified.

Acknowledgements

The publisher and author would like to thank the following people for their co-operation in the production of this book:

Wim Alsemgeest, Montfoort

Firma Bronsema-van Aarle, Zuidbroek

Herman Busser, Gouda

Mr. D. de Jonge, Joure

Gerard de Lange, Joure

Dick Munniksma, Groningen

Succulents Department of Groningen